Durability Testing of an M100-Fueled Toyota LCS-M Carina Equipped with a Resistively Heated Catalytic Converter

U.S. Environmental Protection Agency

The BiblioGov Project is an effort to expand awareness of the public documents and records of the U.S. Government via print publications. In broadening the public understanding of government and its work, an enlightened democracy can grow and prosper. Ranging from historic Congressional Bills to the most recent Budget of the United States Government, the BiblioGov Project spans a wealth of government information. These works are now made available through an environmentally friendly, print-on-demand basis, using only what is necessary to meet the required demands of an interested public. We invite you to learn of the records of the U.S. Government, heightening the knowledge and debate that can lead from such publications.

Included are the following Collections:

Budget of The United States Government
Presidential Documents
United States Code
Education Reports from ERIC
GAO Reports
History of Bills
House Rules and Manual
Public and Private Laws

Code of Federal Regulations
Congressional Documents
Economic Indicators
Federal Register
Government Manuals
House Journal
Privacy act Issuances
Statutes at Large

EPA/AA/CTAB/90-04

Technical Report

Durability Testing Of An M100-Fueled Toyota LCS-M Carina
Equipped With A Resistively Heated Catalytic Converter

by

Gregory K. Piotrowski

September 1990

NOTICE

Technical Reports do not necessarily represent final EPA
decisions or positions. They are intended to present technical
analysis of issues using data which are currently available.
The purpose in the release of such reports is to facilitate the
exchange of technical information and to inform the public of
technical developments which may form the basis for a final EPA
decision, position or regulatory action.

U. S. Environmental Protection Agency
Office of Air and Radiation
Office of Mobile Sources
Emission Control Technology Division
Control Technology and Applications Branch
2565 Plymouth Road
Ann Arbor, Michigan 48105

UNITED STATES ENVIRONMENTAL PROTECTION AGENCY

ANN ARBOR. MICHIGAN 48105

SEP 24 1990

MEMORANDUM

SUBJECT: Exemption From Peer and Administrative Review

FROM: Karl H. Hellman, Chief
Control Technology and Applications Branch

TO: Charles L. Gray, Jr., Director
Emission Control Technology Division

The attached report entitled "Durability Testing Of An M100-Fueled Toyota LCS-M Carina and A Resistively Heated Catalytic Converter" EPA/AA/CTAB/90-04 describes the evaluation of these two systems for exhaust emissions after 6,000 miles of driving over the AMA Durability Driving cycle.

Since this report is concerned only with the presentation of data and its analysis and does not involve matters of policy or regulations, your concurrence is requested to waive administrative review according to the policy outlined in your directive of April 22, 1982.

Concurrence: _____ Date: 9-24-90
Charles L. Gray, Jr., Dir., ECTD

Nonconcurrence: _____ Date: _____
Charles L. Gray, Jr., Dir., ECTD

Attachment

cc: E. Burger, ECTD

Table of Contents

I. Summary

Industry representatives have stated that tailpipe formaldehyde levels from methanol and flexible-fueled vehicles appear to rise significantly in the first 30,000 miles of normal vehicle operation. It has been stated that these emissions typically exceed 15 milligrams per mile in a test over the Federal test procedure (FTP) after 30,000 miles.

An earlier EPA program accumulated 6,000 miles over the AMA durability cycle on an M100-fueled Toyota LCS-M Carina. Formaldehyde levels from this vehicle did not substantially increase during this testing. A resistively heated palladium:cerium catalytic converter was also recently evaluated by EPA. Vehicle formaldehyde emissions were held to a very low 2 milligrams per mile over the FTP with a fresh catalyst.

This mileage accumulation program referred to above was repeated here incorporating both the stock manifold close-coupled platinum:rhodium converter and the resistively heated palladium:cerium converter in an underfloor location. Though the underfloor catalyst was not resistively heated during the mileage accumulation, the goal of this project was to determine the catalyst's ability to reduce formaldehyde emissions over time.

Emissions measured as organic material hydrocarbon equivalent (OMHCE), methanol and carbon monoxide (CO) increased substantially after 6,000 miles were accumulated. OMHCE and CO were measured at 0.09 and 1.90 grams per mile over the Federal test procedure at the end of testing. These levels were still below the current Federally regulated emission levels of these pollutants for methanol-fueled vehicles. Aldehyde emissions rose to 18.8 milligrams per mile over the FTP, up from a low of 3.0 milligrams per mile at the beginning of testing. This level of 18.8 milligrams per mile still represents an efficiency of 97 percent from baseline (no catalyst) with respect to this vehicle.

A severe driveability problem occurred with the test vehicle midway through the project. At that time, the fuel pump, spark plugs, fuel injectors, lean mixture sensor, and engine computer were replaced. The extent to which these problems and the subsequent repairs may have contributed to the increase in emissions over time is unknown.

II. Background

The subject of how emission levels change with accumulated mileage with methanol engine operation has been discussed on numerous occasions between U.S. EPA and automotive industry representatives. Some industry representatives have stated that their research suggests that a significant rise in pollutant emissions occurred suddenly, during the first 5,000-15,000 miles of driving. The nature of this increase was a step-change of considerable magnitude relative to emission levels noted immediately prior to the change. Increases in emissions of unburned fuel and formaldehyde were noted; the vehicles involved were late model, catalyst equipped methanol vehicles.

Toyota Motor Corporation recently published a study of formaldehyde emissions with mileage accumulation on methanol-fueled vehicles.[1] Toyota noted that engine-out formaldehyde emissions, particularly from methanol engines calibrated for lean burn, increased substantially over the first 30,000 miles of driving. Toyota attributed much of this increase to combustion chamber deposits of lubricating oil, and partial oxidation of unburned methanol fuel in the catalytic converter promoted by increases in engine-out NOx emissions. A significant catalyst-out decrease in CO efficiency was noted over 30,000 miles with this study; formaldehyde efficiency decreased from 97 percent to 92 percent after 30,000 miles. Aldehyde emissions from flexible-fueled vehicles (FFV) have been noted to substantially increase as mileage accumulates, when the FFV's are fueled with M85 (85 percent methanol and 15 percent gasoline).[2]

A large increase in emissions from an M100-fueled Volkswagen Rabbit over 15,000 miles of driving at the EPA Motor Vehicle Emissions Laboratory (MVEL) was not noted.[3] This study was limited to an evaluation of engine-out emissions only; a catalyst was not present on the vehicle for the testing.

Another EPA study examined emission level changes with catalyst aging on M85-fueled vehicles.[4] The catalysts were two noble metal formulations at a lighter loading of 20 grams per cubic foot on the substrate.

When tested in a three-way catalyst mode, one formulation exhibited virtually no change in emission levels after aging for 12,000 miles. The second formulation had decreases in efficiency ranging from six percent for emissions measured as hydrocarbons to 40 percent for NOx emissions, over the FTP cycle. A number of factors may have combined to influence the test results and reduce the usefulness of this study, however.[4]

A more recent study of emission levels versus mileage accumulation on a methanol-fueled vehicle involved the accumulation of approximately 6,000 miles on a Toyota Carina equipped with the Toyota Lean Combustion System Methanol (T-LCS-M).[5] The driving was performed under contract at the Bendix test track located in South Bend, Indiana. The driving cycle used for this work was the Federal Durability Driving Schedule.[6] The 6,000 miles were accumulated in two 3,000-mile increments. The vehicle was emission tested by EPA prior to its initial consignment to South Bend. Upon completion of the first 3,000-mile increment, the vehicle was returned to the EPA Motor Vehicle Emission Laboratory (MVEL) in Ann Arbor, Michigan and emission tested. The car was then shipped to South Bend for the second 3,000-mile driving increment. Upon completion of this work, the vehicle was returned to MVEL for further emissions testing.

Emissions measured as hydrocarbons (HC), organic material hydrocarbon equivalents (OMHCE),[7] methanol (CH_3OH), carbon monoxide (CO) and formaldehyde (HCHO) over the FTP cycle did not substantially change during this durability testing. Emission levels of these pollutants at the completion of this project were similar to emission levels from several months prior to its start.

NOx emissions increased slightly over the first 3,000 miles of this project, from 0.89 to 1.01 grams per mile. NOx was measured at a higher level of 1.42 grams per mile at the end of the project. The technicians noted a slight misfire at low-speed cruise conditions during the final 500 miles of mileage accumulation. This condition was not apparent during the emissions testing of the vehicle after it was returned to the EPA laboratory. Immediately after completion of this work, NOx emissions were measured at 1.04 grams per mile during FTP testing conducted with this vehicle.

City and highway fuel economies were essentially unchanged during this project.

EPA has also been concerned about emissions of formaldehyde from methanol-fueled vehicles for some time. The major portion of formaldehyde (HCHO) emissions from a catalyst-equipped methanol-fueled vehicle over the FTP cycle are generated during cold start and warm-up of the catalyst. These emissions are difficult to control because engine-out emissions are high and catalytic converters have low conversion efficiency during their warm-up phase of operation.

Heating the catalytic converter at cold start may provide an emissions reduction benefit over the FTP cycle.[8] Resistively heating a catalytic converter at cold start may be a feasible concept if the electrical power requirement for heating is not excessive and resistive heating is required for only a limited period of time while the vehicle is operated.

Resistively heated metal monolith catalytic converters have been previously evaluated by EPA.[8,9,10,11] The first testing of this technology [9] on a methanol-fueled vehicle utilized a platinum/palladium/rhodium mixture similar to conventional three-way automotive catalysts. FTP Bag 1 levels of emissions measured as hydrocarbons and formaldehyde were 0.50 and 0.054 grams respectively when the catalytic converter was resistively heated for 30 seconds at cold start. These were improvements of 71 and 67 percent respectively over HC and HCHO levels from the same catalyst in the absence of resistive heating. The lower Bag 1 emissions translated into weighted average FTP levels of 0.05 grams per mile for emissions measured as HC and 5 milligrams per mile for HCHO.

Another recent catalyst evaluation program utilized similar resistively heated substates but two different active catalyst formulations.[12,13] These catalysts were:

1.   Palladium, with cerium promoter, and

2.   A base metal composition.

The exact specifications of the catalyst compositions are considered proprietary by the catalyst manufacturers, Camet, Inc. and W. R. Grace. The testing was conducted on a vehicle equipped with a 1.6 liter, 4-cylinder stoichiometrically calibrated engine, fueled with M100.

The Pd:Ce catalyst had the highest emission control efficiencies of either catalyst over the FTP cycle. Emissions measured as organic material hydrocarbon equivalents (OMHCE) were reduced to 0.08 grams per mile, and methanol (CH_3OH) emissions were measured at 0.20 grams per mile with this catalyst. Formaldehyde emissions were reduced to a very low 2 milligrams per mile over the FTP.

The resistively heated catalysts had been evaluated at low mileage only by EPA. Some industry studies referred to previously [1,2] have questioned the ability of the current generation of M85 and flexible fueled vehicles to meet a 15 milligram per mile HCHO standard over the FTP at high mileage. It was decided to repeat the durability testing project involving the M100 Carina vehicle mentioned before, [5] incorporating the resistively heated Pd:Ce catalyst. This project would age the catalyst for 6,000 miles and provide an indication of the catalyst's ability to reduce emissions of formaldehyde over time from a vehicle with high engine-out HCHO emissions.

III. Program Design

This project accumulated 6,000 miles on an M100-fueled test vehicle equipped with a resistively heated Pd:Ce catalytic converter under controlled conditions. The goal of this work was to note any "step change" behavior in HCHO or methanol emissions from the test vehicle during this driving.

The test vehicle was equipped originally with a platinum:rhodium manifold close-coupled catalytic converter; the resistively heated Pd:Ce catalyst was added in an underfloor location. Configured in this manner, the car was tested twice at the MVEL over the FTP and highway fuel economy test (HFET) cycles. The resistively heated catalyst was heated for 10 seconds prior to cold start and 50 seconds following cold start in Bag 1 of the FTP; the catalyst was also heated for 5 seconds prior to hot start and 30 seconds following hot start in Bag 3. No resistive heating was applied during the Bag 2 portion of the FTP or during the HFET cycle tests. The car was then consigned to ATL for the first increment of mileage accumulation.

The driving was performed under contract by ATL at the Bendix test track located in South Bend, Indiana. The 6,000 miles were accumulated in two 3,000-mile increments. The underfloor converter was not resistively heated during the driving at ATL; the catalyst was aged in the absence of resistive heating.

Upon completion of the first 3,000-mile driving increment the car was to be sent to EPA for emissions testing; following this testing, the car was to be returned to ATL for the second 3,000-mile driving increment. After the completion of this second 3,000-mile increment, the car was to be returned to EPA for final emissions testing.

The driving cycle used for the mileage accumulation was the Federal Durability Driving Schedule referred to previously in this report.[6] A description of this driving cycle is given in Appendix A. The engine oil was to be changed at 1,500-mile increments and the waste oil was saved for metals analysis. Results from this testing are presented in the Discussion section.

IV. Test Vehicle Description

The Toyota Lean Combustion System (T-LCS) was described in a paper appearing in the _Japanese Society of Automotive Engineering Review_ (JSAE) July 1984. This system made use of three particular technologies [14] to achieve improvements in fuel economy as well as to comply with NOx emission levels under the Japanese 10-mode cycle:

1.   A lean mixture sensor was used in place of an oxygen sensor to control air/fuel ratio in the lean mixture range;

2.   A swirl control valve before the intake valve was adopted to improve combustion by limiting torque fluctuation at increased air/fuel ratios; and

3.   Sequential fuel injection with optimized injection timing was used to complement the operation of the swirl control valve.

The Toyota Lean Combustion System Methanol (T-LCS-M) is similar to the T-LCS, but has been modified to maximize fuel economy and driving performance while minimizing pollutant emissions through the use of methanol fuel. SAE Paper 860247 [15] describes the development of the T-LCS-M system.

Toyota provided EPA with a T-LCS-M system in a Carina chassis. The Toyota Carina is a right-hand-drive vehicle sold in Japan, but currently not exported to the United States. The power plant is a 1587 cc displacement 4-cylinder, single-overhead camshaft engine. The engine was modified for operation on methanol in a lean-burn mode, incorporating the lean mixture sensor, swirl control valve and timed sequential fuel injection found on the Toyota lean combustion system. Modifications to the fuel system included the substitution of parts resistant to methanol corrosion for stock parts.

Detailed test vehicle specifications are provided in Appendix B.

V.   Catalytic Converter Description

The exhaust system of the test vehicle was equipped with two catalytic converters, a manifold close-coupled converter, and a resistively heated converter mounted in an underfloor location. The close-coupled converter was a Toyota stock converter, utilizing a ceramic monolith substrate. This catalyst was approximately one liter in volume and contained platinum:rhodium in proportion and loading similar to most current OEM three-way catalysts. The underfloor catalyst was a dual bed configuration, consisting of an unheated metal monolith substrate and smaller resistively heated metal monolith. The resistively heated converter was located approximately 39 inches downstream of the outlet of the exhaust manifold.

The metal monolith is resistively heated using a single 12-volt DC battery capable of providing 500-600 cold cranking amps. Voltage measured across the converter during heating was typically 9.0-9.5 volts. Current through the converter was typically measured at 325 and 260 amps at the start and after one minute of resistive heating. The battery used for EPA's testing was an additional battery, not the vehicle's battery, and was located externally to the vehicle.

No resistive heating was applied to the metal monolith during the mileage accumulation at ATL. During emissions testing at the EPA laboratory, the period of resistive heating was limited 10 seconds prior to and 50 seconds following cold start (Bag 1), and 5 seconds prior to and 30 seconds following hot start (Bag 3) in the FTP cycle at 72°F soak conditions.

The dimensions of the underfloor catalyst are similar to those of typical underfloor catalyst(s) on late model automobiles. The amperage draw is comparable to the maximum required by an automotive starter cranking in cold weather, although starter motors generally do not draw this high level of current for as long as the resistively heated catalyst does.

The active catalyst on the resistively heated converter was palladium with cerium promoter. This formulation had been very effective at controlling formaldehyde emissions from a methanol vehicle at low mileage conditions.[12,13]

Further details concerning the characteristics of the resistively heated catalytic converter may be found in publications [9,16,17] and the sales literature [18] of the manufacturer, Camet, Inc., a subsidiary of the W. R. Grace Company.

VI. Test Facilities and Analytical Methods

Emissions testing at EPA was conducted on a Clayton Model ECE-50 double-roll chassis dynamometer, using a direct-drive variable inertia flywheel unit and road load power control unit. The Philco Ford constant volume sampler has a nominal capacity of 350 CFM. Exhaust HC emissions were measured with a Beckman Model 400 flame ionization detector (FID). CO was measured using a Bendix Model 8501-5CA infrared CO analyzer. NOx emissions were determined by a Beckman Model 951A chemiluminescent NOx analyzer.

Exhaust formaldehyde was measured using a dinitrophenyl-hydrazine (DNPH) technique.[19,20] Exhaust carbonyls including formaldehyde are reacted with DNPH solution forming hydrazine derivatives. These derivatives are separated from the DNPH solution by means of high performance liquid chromatography (HPLC), and quantization is accomplished by spectrophotometric analysis of the LC effluent stream.

The procedure developed for methanol sampling and presently in-use employs water-filled impingers through which are pumped a sample of the dilute exhaust or evaporative emissions. The methanol in the sample gas dissolves in water. After the sampling period is complete, the solution in the impingers is analyzed using gas chromatograph (GC) analysis.[21]

VII. Discussion

A.   Emission Test Results

The resistively heated Pd:Ce catalytic converter was placed underfloor on the vehicle exhaust system, and the vehicle was emission tested several times over the FTP and HFET cycles. The Pd:Ce catalyst was resistively heated during portions of the FTP as described earlier; no resistive heating was applied during the HFET testing. Following these initial tests, the vehicle was consigned to ATL for the first increment of mileage accumulation.

Table 1 is a summary of emission test results over the FTP and HFET cycles for this preliminary testing.

The test vehicle had emissions well below currently regulated limits in all categories. Non-methane hydrocarbons (NMHC) were not measured at significantly detectable levels over the FTP. Organic material hydrocarbon equivalents at 0.03 grams per mile were well below the Federal standard of 0.41 grams per mile. Aldehyde emissions in particular were very low, only 3.0 milligrams per mile over the FTP. NOx was the only category of pollutants in which the test vehicle did not have emission levels well below the Federal standard, although the level of the current NOx standard of 1.0 gram per mile was easily met. The only pollutant measured in appreciable concentration under highway driving conditions was NOx, also at approximately 0.7 grams per mile over the HFET.

The mileage accumulation at ATL was conducted over the AMA durability cycle. This driving was conducted without incident for the first 1,000 miles. Several vehicle stalls were noted by the drivers during this time, but the stalls were not considered by the technicians to be serious enough to halt the project. The stalls were noted and the driving continued.

The stalling problem worsened as the driving continued, however. After approximately 1,300 miles of driving, the vehicle stalled on the track and the technicians were unable to immediately restart the engine. It was towed to a garage at the ATL facility where it remained overnight. On the following morning, the vehicle was placed on a chassis dynamometer; the vehicle ran well, with no driveability problems noted. The mileage accumulation work was therefore resumed the next day.

The vehicle was fueled with M100 for this mileage accumulation; no special cold start system was provided. Because of this, vehicle start temperature was limited to a low of approximately 55°F. In order to start the vehicle easily, it was stored in an indoor facility during periods of inactivity. Prior to driving, the vehicle was started indoors and immediately driven onto the test track where the driving was performed.

Table 1

M100 Carina With Two-Catalyst System
Emission Test Results, FTP Cycle
Testing Prior To Initial Vehicle Consignment

Date	HC* (g/mi)	NMHC (g/mi)	OMHCE (g/mi)	CH3OH (g/mi)	CO (g/mi)	NOx (g/mi)	Alde. (mg/mi)
Jan 1990	0.02	0.00	0.03	0.06	0.75	0.70	3.0

HFET Results

Date	HC* (g/mi)	NMHC (g/mi)	OMHCE (g/mi)	CH3OH (g/mi)	CO (g/mi)	NOx (g/mi)	Alde. (mg/mi)
Jan 1990	0.00	0.00	0.00	0.01	0.00	0.69	0.0

---

*   HC measured with propane calibrated FID.

Cold outdoor temperatures were experienced during this testing, which occurred in February 1990. It is possible that these cold ambient conditions adversely affected the driveability of this M100-fueled vehicle. No attempt was made at that time, however, to determine whether cold outdoor temperatures on a particular day affected such parameters as coolant temperature or oil temperature during driving.

At approximately 2,563 miles the stalling problem worsened appreciably. The technicians determined that the vehicle was not sufficiently reliable to ensure completion of the first 3,000-mile driving increment. The vehicle was therefore returned to MVEL on March 12, 1990 for diagnosis and repair.

Only one problem/incident specifically related to the underfloor catalyst was noted during driving at this time. A leak was noted behind the converter. The tailpipe was removed, and a new flange was placed on the pipe to provide a better mating surface to the catalyst flange. The leak had occurred at the downstream joint of the converter.

Upon arrival at MVEL, the vehicle was test driven over the FTP cycle. The stalling problem noted at ATL was also noticed by EPA technicians. On the advice of Toyota engineering personnel, the vehicle fuel tank was drained and the in-tank fuel pump was replaced. This action did not remedy the idle stall problem, however. The fuel injectors were then replaced and the spark plugs cleaned. The vehicle driveability then appeared to have improved enough to conduct emissions testing.

A sample of the fuel in the vehicle tank was taken when the tank was drained for the replacement of the pump. This sample was tested twice at MVEL for water content under ASTM standard "Test Method for Determination of C_1 to C_4 Alcohols and MTBE in Gasoline Using Gas Chromatography" (D4818-88) Vol. 5.01, 1988. The samples should have consisted of nearly 100 percent alcohol due to the use of M100 fuel. Instead, alcohol contents of 85 and 88 percent respectively were measured for the two samples.

The remainder of the fuel sample was sent to a contract laboratory for Karl Fischer titration analysis (ASTM D1744). We were concerned that possible water contamination of the fuel might have occurred. The analysis indicated only 511 ppm water content in the fuel, however.

It is possible that fuel contamination or even misfueling might have occurred during the mileage accumulation, based on the above. Very little fuel remained in the ATL M100 supply when the test vehicle was returned to EPA. New M100 was ordered at this time, and the remaining fuel was disposed of. We were unable, therefore, to sample the M100 used by ATL when the driveability problems arose.

Table 2 contains a summary of the testing over the FTP cycle performed at 2,563 miles into this project. The first category under "Description of Testing" is a test with no resistive heating applied to the catalyst, after the replacement of the fuel pump and injectors. The second category repeats this testing with the underfloor catalyst resistively heated as described earlier.

Resistive heating significantly increased the efficiency of the underfloor catalyst with respect to methanol, HC and formaldehyde emissions. These emissions are reduced roughly 50 percent by catalyst resistive heating. CO was not affected by catalyst resistive heating. Even with a lean burn methanol-fueled vehicle, it may be necessary to add additional air in front of the converter to reduce CO levels during warm up.[11] The reduction in NOx levels was unexpected given our previous experience with this heated converter.[12,13]

The emission levels of most measured pollutants appeared to have significantly changed from the start of the program to the 2,563-mile point. Most emission levels appeared to have doubled with CO and aldehyde emissions increasing more than 100 percent. The aldehyde increase, from 3.0 milligrams per mile increasing to 8.3 milligrams per mile, was most noticeable.

During this testing another driveability problem was noted by the EPA technicians. Stalls in the latter part of the FTP (Bags 2 and 3) were noticed, occurring two to three times per test. Though these stalls were not occurring during the most critical portion of the test with respect to emissions (Bag 1 cold start), it was possible that this driveability problem might have materially affected the emissions profile. The problem was described to Toyota, and their assistance with diagnosis and repair was again requested.

Toyota provided EPA with a new lean burn sensor and computer PROM for the Carina vehicle. These parts were installed, and the driveability problems ceased. The FTP tests were repeated with the underfloor catalyst resistively heated as referred to previously. The third category in Table 2 provides results from this testing.

Emissions of HC, methanol and aldehydes did not change significantly as a result of these latest modifications. Emissions of CO and NOx however, decreased approximately 40 and 50 percent respectively, from levels measured immediately before the lean burn sensor and PROM were replaced.

Table 3 contains data in grams per Bag 1 from FTP testing with the underfloor catalyst resistively heated. Testing prior to mileage accumulation is described together with testing at 2,563 miles after replacement of the fuel injectors and fuel pump, and finally after replacement of the lean burner sensor and engine computer.

Table 2

M100 Carina With Two Catalyst System
Emission Test Results, FTP Cycle
Testing At 2,563 Miles

Description of Testing	HC* (g/mi)	NMHC (g/mi)	OMHCE (g/mi)	CH3OH (g/mi)	CO (g/mi)	NOx (g/mi)	Alde. (mg/mi)
New pump, injectors, no resistive heat	0.11	0.01	0.15	0.26	2.04	0.97	20.3
New pump, injectors, resistive heat to catalyst	0.05	0.00	0.07	0.13	2.14	0.66	8.3
New pump, injectors, LB sensor, ECU, resistive heat to catalyst	0.05	0.00	0.06	0.11	1.34	0.34	8.5

* HC measured with propane calibrated FID.

Table 3

Bag 1 Emissions From FTP Cycle
FTP Cycle, Testing at 2,563 Miles

Description of Testing*	HC** (g/bag)	NMHC (g/bag)	OMHCE (g/bag)	CH3OH (g/bag)	CO (g/bag)	NOx (g/bag)	Alde (mg/ba
Prior to mileage accumulation	0.25	0.04	0.33	0.55	9.39	2.85	33.
2,563 miles, new pump, injectors	0.58	0.04	0.79	1.42	15.81	2.66	111.
2,563 miles, new pump, injectors, sensor, ECU	0.66	0.11	0.87	1.47	14.08	1.92	109.

*   Underfloor catalyst resistively heated.

**   HC measured with propane calibrated FID.

The trends in emissions in Bag 1 follow those for the weighted FTP noted earlier. Emissions measured as organic material hydrocarbon equivalents, methanol and aldehydes in Bag 1 increased significantly after 2,563 miles. The replacement of the lean burn sensor and engine computer did not significantly effect tailpipe emissions over Bag 1. CO and NOx Bag 1 levels appeared to be reduced slightly by the replacement of these components.

Driveability was much improved as a result of these final changes; the stalling problem, either at hot or cold idle, was not noticed. The driveability had improved enough to permit the completion of the durability driving, so the vehicle was returned to the ATL facility.

Driving continued at the test track without serious incident, the only driveability concern being an occasional stall followed by a quick restart. The vehicle was returned to MVEL following the completion of the mileage accumulation at the end of June 1990.

Table 4 contains a summary of the test data prior to the start of driving, at the 2,563-mile point, and at the completion of the project. Emissions measured as NMHC, OMHCE, and of methanol are presented in graphical form in Figure 1. Figure 2 presents the same information for CO, NOx and aldehyde emissions. Aldehyde emissions, in milligrams per mile, have been divided by a factor of 10 for easier inclusion on Figure 2. The testing at the 2,563-mile point referred to was conducted after all of the diagnostic and repair work referred to previously was completed. No attempt is made to determine the effect of these repairs on the comparability of emission levels between the 2,500-mile point and the completion of the project.

NMHC emissions, possibly associated primarily with lube oil emissions, were uniformly low throughout the duration of the project. Emissions of OMHCE and methanol steadily increased with accumulated mileage, however. Emissions of CO increased steadily over time also; after the repair work, CO levels continued to increase. NOx was reduced to a low of about 0.4 grams per mile at the time of the engine repairs; this level increased to approximately 0.5 grams per mile at the end of the project. Aldehydes increased steadily, exceeding 18 milligrams per mile over the FTP at the end of the project. The 18.8 milligrams per mile level at the end of testing exceeds the 15 milligrams per mile standard for model year 1993 methanol vehicles proposed by the California Air Resources Board.[22] The 18.8 milligrams per mile over the FTP still represents an efficiency of 97 percent with respect to baseline emissions of 570 milligrams per mile with this vehicle.[23]

Table 4

Emission Test Results, FTP Cycle
Summary After Completion of Testing

Test Date	HC* (g/mi)	NMHC (g/mi)	OMHCE (g/mi)	CH3OH (g/mi)	CO (g/mi)	NOx (g/mi)	Alde. (mg/mi)
Jan 1990 start of testing	0.02	0.00	0.03	0.06	0.75	0.70	3.0
April 1990 2,563 miles	0.05	0.00	0.06	0.11	1.34	0.34	8.5
May 1990 6,000 miles	0.07	0.01	0.09	0.16	1.90	0.48	18.8

HFET Results

Test Date	HC* (g/mi)	NMHC (g/mi)	OMHCE (g/mi)	CH3OH (g/mi)	CO (g/mi)	NOx (g/mi)	Alde. (mg/mi)
Jan 1990	0.00	0.00	0.00	0.01	0.00	0.69	0.0
April 1990	0.00	0.00	0.00	0.01	0.03	0.14	0.5
May 1990	0.00	0.00	0.01	0.01	0.09	0.22	1.7

---

*   HC measured with propane calibrated FID.

Figure 1
M100 Carina With Heated Catalyst
Emission Results, FTP Cycle

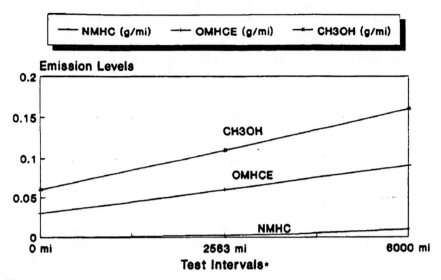

• Not to scale

Figure 2
M100 Carina With Heated Catalyst
Emission Results, FTP Cycle

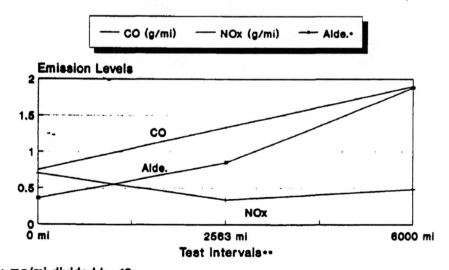

• mg/mi divided by 10
•• Not to scale

The general increase in pollutant emissions noted here could have been caused by a number of factors. For example, the driveability problems noted earlier could be a source of higher HC and CO emissions. It is possible that other problems, not identified during the diagnostic and repair work performed midway in the project, contributed to the higher emissions noted at the end of the project. A new methanol-tolerant fuel pump will soon be supplied to EPA by Toyota. Toyota believes that the replacement pump presently on the Carina may be subject to deterioration that would adversely affect the performance of the engine.

Deterioration of the catalytic converter systems could also have occurred and caused an increase in pollutant emission levels. This deterioration could have occurred in several different ways. For example, the manifold close-coupled converter could have been subjected to significant thermal shock if engine misfire occurred. A small amount of black carbon matter was found on the face of the resistively heated catalytic converter after the project. It is possible that conditions in front of the converter together with the choice of active catalyst combined to induce coking. This reaction would be detrimental to the catalyst, eventually poisoning and deactivating it.

Figures 3 and 4 give FTP emissions over time for several pollutant categories for the M100 Carina equipped with the stock manifold close-coupled catalyst. The testing reported was conducted without utilizing the resistively heated underfloor Pd:Ce converter. The testing referred to as August 1990 was conducted after the completion of the mileage accumulation program.

In general, emissions from the test vehicle have approximately doubled during the last 8,000 miles of driving (much of this mileage being the durability work reported on here). Emissions measured as OMHCE and methanol more than doubled during this time, to 0.19 and 0.34 grams per mile. Formaldehyde emissions roughly doubled to 25 milligrams per mile. CO emissions have quadrupled from the December 1986 levels. NOx emissions are presently at approximately similar levels to those when the car was first received from Toyota in 1986. During this time, NOx has varied from a high of 1.42 grams per mile in June 1990. These swings may have been caused in large part by modifications and engine repairs to correct perceived driveability problems.

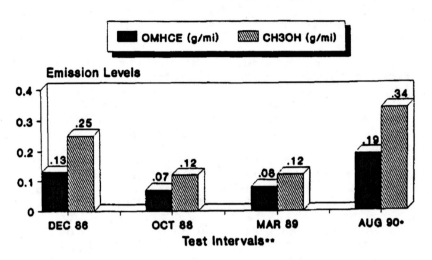

Figure 3
M100 Carina Without Camet Catalyst
Emission Results, FTP Cycle

• Denotes end of current effort
•• Not to scale

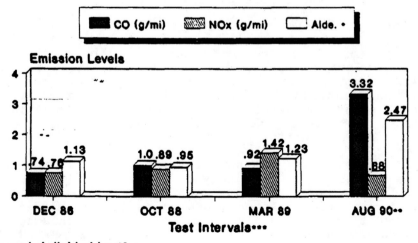

Figure 4
M100 Carina Without Camet Catalyst
Emission Results, FTP Cycle

• mg/mi divided by 10
•• Denotes end of current effort
••• Not to scale

At present, it is difficult to determine quantitatively what portion of the recent increase in emission levels is due to mechanical troubles yet occurring with the vehicle. The fuel pump on the vehicle will be replaced with a new methanol-tolerant pump when it is received from Toyota. Subsequent emissions testing will indicate whether this component was a cause of higher emission levels.

One way to determine whether the resistively heated underfloor catalyst had deteriorated and contributed to higher emissions is to test this catalyst on a vehicle other than the LCS-M Carina. The same resistively heated Pd:Ce converter had been evaluated on a stoichiometrically calibrated M100-fueled vehicle just prior to the work described in this report. The results from testing on this stoichiometrically calibrated vehicle have been previously reported.[12,13] This previous testing was recent enough to attempt a comparison of results from previous and current testing. In addition, the stoichiometrically calibrated vehicle had not been used for a project since the testing described in [12,13]; no modifications had been made to the vehicle, nor had it been operated under severe conditions.

The stoichiometrically calibrated vehicle was a 1981 Volkswagen Rabbit sedan equipped with a 1.6 liter engine and fueled with M100. The characteristics of this vehicle are given in detail in [12]. The resistively heated Pd:Ce catalyst was removed from the Carina and placed on the Rabbit in the same underfloor location as the testing described in [12,13]. The Rabbit was emission tested twice over the FTP cycle. The catalyst was resistively heated in the same manner as described in this earlier testing [12,13] and in this report. Results from this current testing are compared with testing conducted on this vehicle in December 1989 in Table 5. Test results over the FTP cycle are presented, together with emission levels in grams from the Bag 1 portion of the tests.

Current levels of OMHCE and CH_3OH were much higher than the very low levels measured during December 1989. At 0.29 grams per mile, current OMHCE were still below the 0.41 grams per mile level mandated in the Federal light-duty methanol vehicle regulations. CO was still below the Federally regulated emission levels of 3.4 grams per mile, but the current emissions level was three times the magnitude of the December 1989 level. NOx also rose slightly, to 1.0 gram per mile during the current testing.

The emissions category showing the greatest percentage increase over time was aldehyde. Very low aldehyde emissions of 2.0 milligrams per mile were measured with this catalyst when it was fresh. After 6,000 miles on the M100-fueled lean burn vehicle, the catalyst was capable of reducing aldehyde emission levels to only 33 milligrams per mile over the FTP.

Table 5

M100 Volkswagen Rabbit With Camet
Pd:Ce Converter Emissions Testing, FTP Test Cycle

Date	NMHC (g/mi)	OMHCE (g/mi)	CH3OH (g/mi)	CO (g/mi)	NOx (g/mi)	Alde. (mg/mi)
December 1989	0.01	0.08	0.20	0.6	0.7	2.0
August 1990	0.02	0.29	0.55	1.8	1.0	33.3

Bag 1 Only

Date	NMHC (g)	OMHCE (g)	CH3OH (g)	CO (g)	NOx (g)	Alde. (mg)
December 1989	0.04	1.19	2.94	9.1	3.3	29.5
August 1990	0.37	3.98	7.76	18.3	5.2	406.2

Bag 1 emissions were uniformly higher when the most recent tests were compared to testing with a fresh catalyst. OMHCE emissions during the most recent testing were over three times as high as testing during December 1989. Aldehyde emissions in particular had increased in magnitude significantly, to approximately 406 mg over Bag 1.

No driveability problems with the Volkswagen Rabbit were noted during the August 1990 testing; the car performed very well. No problems with catalyst resistive heating were noted during this testing. Baseline (no-catalyst) emission levels were not measured during August 1990, because there were no comparable emissions data available from December 1989.

The resistively heated Pd:Ce catalyst was removed from the Rabbit vehicle following the completion of testing and returned to W. R. Grace. This catalyst will be analyzed by Grace to determine whether catalyst deterioration has occurred, and if so, what the mechanism of deactivation was.

B.   Fuel Economy Testing

Fuel economy test results are presented in Table 6. City, highway, and composite methanol MPG figures are presented as well as gasoline equivalent composite fuel economy. Fuel economy data is in chronological order, since the test vehicle was received from Toyota, Japan, is also presented for comparison.

The gasoline equivalent fuel economy values are based on adjusting for the energy content difference between gasoline and methanol. The nominal energy content of gasoline has been established at 18,507 BTU/lb [24] yielding 114,132 BTU/gallon. Methanol at 8,600 BTU/lb is 56,768 BTU/gallon. The adjustment for M100 fuel based on fuel energy is:

Gasoline equivalent adjustment = $\dfrac{\text{Energy of gasoline}}{\text{Energy of methanol}}$

Dividing the energy of gasoline:

Gasoline equivalent adjustment = 2.0105

FTP fuel economy was essentially unchanged from previous levels by this project. Fuel economy increased slightly during the project from 18.3 MPG over the FTP at project start to 19.0 MPG at the completion. This 19.0 methanol MPG was the highest city fuel economy measured to date with the test vehicle, but this was only 0.3 MPG higher than the values recorded when the vehicle was first delivered to EPA. We do not know the effect on fuel economy of each of the modifications that were made to the vehicle midway in the project (replacement of plugs, lean mixture sensor, ECU, and fuel pump).

Table 6

Toyota LCS-M Carina
Fuel Economy Test Results

Date	City MPG	Highway MPG	Composite MPG	Gasoline Equivalent Composite MPG
September 1986	18.7	N/A	N/A	N/A
December 1986	17.9	25.7	20.7	41.6
July 1987	17.0	24.4	19.7	39.6
July 1988	18.2	23.7	20.3	40.8
October 1988	18.6	26.5	21.5	43.2
March 1989	18.0	25.4	20.7	41.6
January 1990*	18.3	26.1	21.1	42.4
May 1990**	18.6	26.2	21.4	43.0
June 1990***	19.0	27.3	22.0	44.2

---

*   Start of current program.

**   Midway point of current program.

***   End of current program.

Highway fuel economy appears to follow city MPG. A small, yet measurable increase in highway fuel economy was noted over the current project. The 27.3 MPG highway fuel economy at the end of the project combined with the higher 19.0 methanol city MPG to give a gasoline equivalent composite fuel economy of 44.2 MPG. While this was the highest gasoline equivalent composite fuel economy yet recorded with this vehicle, it was yet only marginally higher than the 43.2 MPG measured in October 1988.

C.   Lubricant Analysis

Published reports have indicated that the use of methanol fuel may result in engine wear rates that exceed those of comparably sized gasoline engine, when conventional lubricants are used.[25,26] Typically, this increased wear is described as having occurred in the top piston ring and upper cylinder bore area.[27]

Toyota specified an oil change interval of 3,000 miles when the Carina was delivered to EPA for evaluation. During a previous mileage accumulation effort involving this vehicle, the oil was changed every 1,500 miles and analyzed for wear metals content.[5] For the effort described here, the engine oil was also to be changed at 1,500-mile intervals and samples were to be taken for metal content.

The first sample was taken after 1,500 miles had been driven. The vehicle had been driven for an additional 850 miles prior to the start of the program, for a total of 2,350 miles with the same oil. We chose to not change the oil at the beginning of the program to determine what the effect of a more normal oil change interval would be on contaminant metals concentrations.

The second oil sample was taken after the vehicle was returned to MVEL for engine diagnostics and repair. A complete 1,500-mile increment was not driven between the first oil change and the return of the vehicle to MVEL. It proved convenient to change the oil while the vehicle was at MVEL, so this sample is referred to here as being taken after only 1,063 miles of driving on the oil that was sampled.

The third sample was taken after a cumulative total of 4,500 miles had been driven on the vehicle during the project. This third sample therefore was taken after approximately 1,936 miles had been accumulated since the second sample. The fourth and final sample was drawn after the final 1,500-mile driving increment.

The oil samples were analyzed from FRAM through their FRAM/CODE oil analysis program. This analysis includes a spectrographic metals test as well as a series of physical tests to determine viscosity, fuel dilution and solids content of the oil. This information was used as an indicator to determine whether abnormal wear of parts was occurring.

Results from analyzing these individual oil samples are presented in Table 7. The wear metals data presented here was limited to those metals which indicated higher than normal parts wear or related to major engine components.[28] The FRAM program made the determination that higher than normal wear was occurring.

The wear metals data is presented in two formats. First, wear metals content of the sample taken is presented in units of parts per million (ppm) by weight. Because the oil was sampled after different driving intervals and the oil was changed when sampled, this length of driving time may have influenced the metals content of the oil. For example, the first sample was taken after 2,358 miles of driving, and the oil was changed at sampling time. Barring unusual driving conditions or engine trouble, it may be logical to expect that the metals content of the second sample, taken after driving 1,063 miles, might be lower due to the shorter period of wear. The data is therefore presented also in terms of ppm of metal per mile driven with the oil sampled at that time.

Oil sample number 2 exhibited somewhat different levels of wear metals per mile than the other samples. This situation may have been related to the driveability problems which became very noticeable at that time. Water contamination of the oil was noticed at this time; this contamination was not noticed in the other samples taken. The source of this water contamination is unknown. This could have been caused by fuel contamination, excessive blowby, or cold ambient temperatures which may have hindered the functioning of the PCV system. The following two oil samples indicated less wear generally with respect to the number of miles traveled with the same oil. For these reasons, the second oil sample may not be a good indicator of the average wear metals levels to the expected from a methanol-vehicle under normal wear conditions.

Higher than normal concentrations of iron were indicated in three of the four oil samples. Higher concentrations of iron are normally present where increased wear in the cylinders and of gears is occurring. Elevated levels of aluminum were also found in the same three samples. Aluminum is generally present in oil due to wear of pistons and bearing surfaces.

Table 7

Metal Contaminants In Lube Oil Samples
(data given in PPM and PPM/mile)

Metal/Other Contaminant	Sample 1 2,358 miles	Sample 2 1,063 miles	Sample 3 1,936 miles	Sample 4 1,500 miles
Iron	72*/0.031	67*/0.063	75*/0.039	37/0.025
Aluminum	20*/0.008	13*/0.012	18*/0.009	6/0.004
Chromium	22*/0.009	22*/0.021	30*/0.015	17/0.011
Copper	6 /0.003	4 /0.004	4 /0.002	2/0.001
Lead	37*/0.016	25*/0.024	14 /0.007	16/0.011
Water	--	0.1**	--	--

*   Levels flagged by FRAM as of moderate concern.

**   Water level greater than 0.1 volume percent measured.

Elevated concentrations of chromium, probably from piston rings, were noted in the first three oil samples. Higher than normal concentrations of lead were also noted in the first two samples. Because of the use of M100, the lead probably was not related to the fuel vapors. Higher levels of lead, when accompanied by elevated concentrations of aluminum, may be an indicator of bearing wear. Copper levels, however, were within the range considered to be normal by FRAM; copper is also commonly associated with bearing surfaces.

Pefley, in SAE Paper 831704, [29] provides oil analysis wear metals data from a small fleet of methanol-fueled sedans. These vehicles were powered by 1.6-liter Volkswagen engines; vehicle weight and engine displacement were similar to the Toyota Carina test vehicle used in this project. The oil used in Pefley's work was a commercially available SAE 20W-40 SF-CC oil. The oil was sampled every 1,000 miles and was changed at 3,000-mile intervals. Pefley's vehicles were driven from 7,000 to 17,000 miles; oil sampling did not occur during the first 3,000 miles of break-in driving. Numerical averages of Pefley's wear metals data are presented in Figures 5 and 6.

Also presented in Figures 5 and 6 is wear metals data from the previous 6,000-mile durability effort with this test vehicle.[5] These samples were taken at 1,500-mile increments; the driving was conducted over the same driving schedule as the present effort described here. The oil used in this earlier testing was the same specially blended lubricant for methanol-fueled vehicles. Figures 5 and 6 also contain wear metals data from the first, third, and fourth samples taken during the current effort. The data from the second sample is not included here, as this sample was taken when the vehicle was experiencing obvious driveability problems. The data presented in Figures 5 and 6 is limited to metals concentrations in ppm as presented in the earlier reports quoted from here.[5,29]

The iron concentrations measured during the present testing were roughly comparable to the levels measured during the earlier durability effort [5] if the extended driving of the first two samples is considered. The last sample, 37 ppm, is a considerable improvement over the 49 ppm average measured during.[5] All of the samples from the M100-fueled Toyota vehicle had much lower iron levels in their oil than the methanol-fueled Volkswagen vehicles used by Pefley.[29]

Aluminum concentrations from the first and third samples of the current effort were similar in magnitude to those of the previous durability effort [5] when the mileage over 1,500 miles is considered. The last sample of the current effort was taken after driving 1,500 miles; at 6 ppm, this concentration of aluminum was less than one half of that measured during the previous durability experiments.[5] The methanol-fueled Volkswagen vehicles used in SAE Paper 831704 exhibited considerably higher aluminum wear metals concentration than on the M100 Toyota vehicle.

Figure 5
Oil Analysis - Metal Contamination
Comparison With Published Data

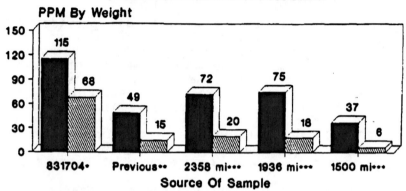

* From SAE 831704
** From CTAB 89-03
*** Present Work Described Here

Figure 6
Oil Analysis - Metal Contamination
Comparison With Published Data

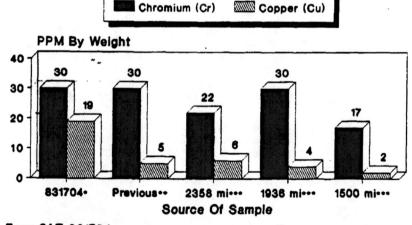

* From SAE 831704
** From CTAB 89-03
*** Present Work Described Here

Chromium levels in oil from Carina testing could not be correlated with miles driven on the same oil. The 30 ppm of chromium measured with the oil used for 1,936 miles was higher than the 22 ppm measured in oil that was run in the engine for 2,358 miles. The final 1,500-mile sample taken during the present work had a chromium concentration of only 17 ppm. This was considerably below most other measured levels and the data presented in SAE Paper 831704.

Concentrations of copper were measured at relatively low levels during the present work as well as during the past durability project.[5] Though copper concentrations appeared to increase with increasing mileage experienced by the oil during the present work, the final sample over 1,500 miles had less than half the level measured for 1,500 miles in the previous project. The copper concentration of 2 ppm from this final sample was also substantially below the 19 ppm measured by Pefley during his work.

No attempt to relate metals wear rates to engine condition or emissions is made here. We did not examine the condition of cylinder walls, bearing surfaces, piston crowns, etc. either before or after the current effort. A limited number of oil analyses were made, and these did not occur at evenly spaced intervals. Gasoline control vehicles were not used and the analysis was limited to a single test vehicle. The data presented here suggests that some accelerated engine wear with respect to expected gasoline vehicle wear may be occurring in the test vehicle, according to FRAM. While the possibility of advanced wear rates should be a concern of those responsible for methanol vehicle fleets, no attempt was made to reduce them here, through the use of special lubricant additives or special methanol-tolerant metal surfaces.

VIII. Test Highlights

1.   Emissions of OMHCE, CH₃OH, and CO over the FTP increased substantially after 6,000 miles of driving over the AMA durability cycle. OMHCE at 0.09 and CO at 1.90 grams per mile at the end of testing were still below current Federally regulated emission levels for methanol vehicles.

2.   NOx emissions over the FTP dropped to a very low 0.34 grams per mile after a driveability problem was investigated and corrected midway in the program.

3.   Aldehyde emissions rose to 18.8 milligrams per mile at the end of testing, up from a very low 3.0 milligrams per mile at the start of the program. This 18.8 milligrams per mile over the FTP still represents an efficiency of 97 percent from baseline with respect to this vehicle.

4. City and highway fuel economies were essentially unchanged by the project. The gasoline equivalent composite fuel economy of 44.2 MPG measured at the end of testing was similar to the 43.2 MPG measured during October 1988.

5. Oil samples were taken four times from the test vehicle during this project and analyzed for wear metals concentrations. According to FRAM, Inc. standards, three of the samples indicated higher than normal concentrations of iron, aluminum, and chromium. Lead concentrations were judged by FRAM to be higher than normal in two samples. A significant amount of water was found to be present in the lube oil during a period in which severe driveability problems with the test vehicle were noted.

The extent to which out of the ordinary driveability problems may have affected these wear metals concentrations is unknown. The final sample, taken after 1,500 miles of relatively incident-free driving, showed normal concentrations of the metals mentioned above; no category was flagged as indicative of abnormal wear rates. More testing over a longer period of vehicle operation should be conducted to determine whether this methanol-fueled engine is experiencing metal wear rates higher than those expected from a comparable gasoline-fueled engine.

IX. Acknowledgments

The Toyota Carina test vehicle was loaned to EPA for use with alternative fuels research programs by the Toyota Motor Co., Ltd. The M100-fueled Rabbit vehicle has been loaned to EPA by Volkswagen of America. The resistively heated catalyst was provided by Camet, Inc., a subsidiary of W. R. Grace. FRAM, Inc., a subsidiary of Allied Signal, provided the lubricant analysis. The engine oil, specially blended for use with methanol vehicles, was provided by Lubrizol.

The author appreciates the efforts of James Garvey, Robert Moss, and Steve Halfyard of the Test and Evaluation Branch (TEB) who conducted the emissions testing and assisted with the driveability problem diagnosis and repair. John Shelton, also of TEB, acted as the EPA contract officer and liason with ATL for this effort.

X. References

1. "Study of Mileage-Related Formaldehyde Emission from Methanol-Fueled Vehicles," Tsukasaki, Y., et al., SAE Paper 900705, February 1990.

2. "A View of Flexible Fuel Vehicle Aldehyde Emissions," Nichols, R. J., et al., SAE Paper 881200, August 1988.

3. Results of Methanol Catalyst Testing Analyzed for Trends In Baseline Variance, Memorandum, Piotrowski, G. K., OAR/OMS/ECTD/CTAB, October 24, 1985.

4. "Durability of Low Cost Catalysts for Methanol-Fueled Vehicles," Heavenrich, R. M., R. I. Bruetsch, and G. K. Piotrowski, EPA/AA/CTAB/87-01, October 1987.

5. "Durability Testing of a Toyota LCS-M Carina," Piotrowski, G. K., EPA/AA/CTAB/89-03, June 1989.

6. Federal Durability Driving Schedule, Appendix IV, Part 86, 40 CFR, Chapter 1.

7. Definitions, 40 CFR Part 86.092-2, Federal Register, Vol. 54, No. 68, Tuesday, April 11, 1989.

8. "Resistive Materials Applied to Quick Light-Off Catalysts," SAE Paper 890799, Hellman, K. H., et al., March 1989.

9. "Evaluation of a Resistively Heated Metal Monolith Catalytic Converter on an M100 Neat Methanol-Fueled Vehicle," Blair, D. M. and G. K. Piotrowski, EPA/AA/CTAB/88-08, August 1988.

10. "Evaluation of a Resistively Heated Metal Monolith Catalytic Converter on a Gasoline-Fueled Vehicle," Piotrowski, G. K., EPA/AA/CTAB/88-12, December 1988.

11. "A Resistively Heated Catalytic Converter With Air Injection For Oxidation of Carbon Monoxide and Hydrocarbons At Reduced Ambient Temperatures," Piotrowski, G. K., EPA/AA/CTAB/89-06, September 1989.

12. "Evaluation of Resistively Heated Metal Monolith Catalytic Converters On An M100 Neat Methanol-Fueled Vehicle," Part II, Piotrowski, G. K., EPA/AA/CTAB/89-09, December 1989.

13. "Recent Results from Prototype Vehicle and Emission Control Technology Evaluation Using Methanol Fuel," SAE Paper 901112, Hellman, K. H. and G. K. Piotrowski, May 1990.

14.   "NOx Reduction Is Compatible With Fuel Economy Through Toyota's Lean Combustion System," Kimbara, Y. K., et al., SAE Paper 851210, October 1985.

15.   "Development of Methanol Lean Burn System," Katoh, K., Y. Imamura, and T. Inoue, SAE Paper 860247, February 1986.

16.   "Recent Developments in Electrically Heated Metal Monoliths," Whittenberger, W. A. and J. E. Kubsh, SAE Paper 900503, February 1990.

17.   "Evaluation of Metallic and Electrically Heated Metallic Catalysts on a Gasoline-Fueled Vehicle," Hurley, R. G., et al., SAE Paper 900504, February 1990.

18.   "Camet Electrically Heated Catalytic Converter," Sales Literature, Camet Company, 12000 Winrock Road, Hiram, Ohio, 44234, February 1990.

19.   Formaldehyde Measurement In Vehicle Exhaust at MVEL, Memorandum, Gilkey, R. L., OAR/OMS/EOD, Ann Arbor, MI, 1981.

20.   "Formaldehyde Sampling From Automobile Exhaust: A Hardware Approach," Pidgeon, W., EPA/AA/TEB/88-01, July 1988.

21.   "Sample Preparation Techniques For Evaluating Methanol and Formaldehyde Emissions From Methanol-Fueled Vehicles and Engines," Pidgeon, W. and M. Reed, EPA/AA/TEB/ 88-02, September 1988.

22.   "Proposed Regulations For Low-Emission Vehicles and Clean Fuels," Staff Report, State of California Air Resources Board, August 13, 1990.

23.   "Evaluation of Toyota LCS-M Carina: Phase II," Piotrowski, G. K., EPA/AA/CTAB/87-09, December 1987.

24.   Federal Register, Vol. 50, No. 126, p. 27179, July 1, 1985.

25.   "The Mechanisms Leading to Increased Wear In Methanol Fueled SI Engines," Ryan, T. W., et al., SAE Paper 811200, October 1981.

26.   "Lubrication Experience In Methanol-Fueled Engines Under Short-Trip Service Conditions," Chamberlin, W. B. and W. C. Brandon, SAE Paper 831701, November 1983.

27.   "The Effects of Lubricant Composition on SI Engine Wear With Alcohol Fuels," Marbach, H. W., et al., SAE Paper 831702, November 1983.

28.   The   FRAM/CODE   Oil   Analysis   program,"   Sales
Literature,   Allied   Automotive   Aftermarket   Division,   Allied
Signal, East Providence, RI, 1990.

29.   "Methanol Engine Durability," Ernst, R. J., R. K.
Pefley, and F. J. Weins, SAE Paper 831704, November 1983.

APPENDIX A

DESCRIPTION OF TOYOTA LCS-M TEST VEHICLE

The Durability Driving Schedule for light-duty vehicles consists of 11 laps of a 3.7-mile course. The basic vehicle speed for each lap is given below.

Table A-1

Basic Lap Speed
Durability Driving Schedule

Lap	Speed (miles per hour)
1	40
2	30
3	40
4	40
5	35
6	30
7	35
8	45
9	35
10	55
11	70

Each of the first nine laps contain four steps with 15-second idle periods. These laps also contain five light decelerations from base speed to 20 miles per hour followed by light accelerations to the base speed. The tenth lap is run at a constant speed of 55 miles per hour. The eleventh lap is begun with wide-open throttle acceleration from stop to 70 miles per hour. A normal deceleration to idle followed by a second wide-open throttle acceleration occurs at the midpoint of the lap.

Figure A-1 below is a diagram of one lap of the Durability Driving Schedule taken from 40 CFR, Chapter 1, Part 86, Appendix IV.

Figure A-1

Durability Driving Schedule Lap

[From 40 CFR, Chapter 1, Part 86, Appendix IV]

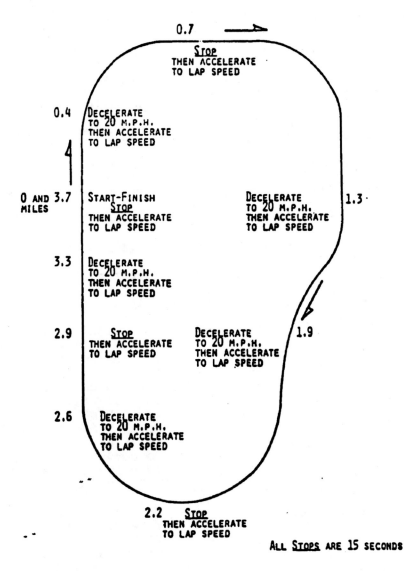

0.7

STOP
THEN ACCELERATE
TO LAP SPEED

0.4 DECELERATE
TO 20 M.P.H.
THEN ACCELERATE
TO LAP SPEED

0 AND 3.7   START-FINISH
MILES   STOP
             THEN ACCELERATE
             TO LAP SPEED

DECELERATE
TO 20 M.P.H.
THEN ACCELERATE
TO LAP SPEED   1.3

3.3 DECELERATE
TO 20 M.P.H.
THEN ACCELERATE
TO LAP SPEED

1.9

2.9   STOP
THEN ACCELERATE
TO LAP SPEED

DECELERATE
TO 20 M.P.H.
THEN ACCELERATE
TO LAP SPEED

2.6 DECELERATE
TO 20 M.P.H.
THEN ACCELERATE
TO LAP SPEED

2.2 STOP
THEN ACCELERATE
TO LAP SPEED

ALL STOPS ARE 15 SECONDS

APPENDIX B

DESCRIPTION OF TOYOTA LCS-M TEST VEHICLE

Vehicle weight	2015 lbs
Test weight	2250 lbs
Transmission	Manual, 5 speed
Shift speed code	15-25-40-45 mph
Fuel	M100 neat methanol
Number of cylinders	Four, in-line
Displacement	97 cubic inches
Camshaft	Single, overhead camshaft
Compression ratio	11.5, flat-head pistons
Combustion chamber	Wedge shape
Fuel Metering	Electronic port fuel injection
Bore and Stroke	3.19 inches x 3.03 inches
Ignition	Spark ignition; spark plugs are ND W27ESR-U, gapped at .8 mm, torqued to 13 ft-lb.
Ignition timing	With check connecter shorted, ignition timing should be set to 10°BTDC at idle. With check connecter unshorted, ignition timing advance should be set to 15°BTDC at idle. Idle speed is approximately 550-700 rpm.
Fuel injectors	Main and cold start fuel injectors capable of high fuel flow rates. The fuel injector bodies have been nickel-plated, and the adjusting pipes are stainless steel.

DESCRIPTION OF TOYOTA LCS-M TEST VEHICLE

Fuel pump

In-tank electric fuel pump with brushless motor to prevent corrosion. The body is nickel plated and its fuel delivery flow rate capacity has been increased.

Fuel tank

Stainless steel construction; capacity 14.5 gals.

Fuel lines and filter

The tube running from the fuel tank to the fuel filter has been nickel plated. The fuel filter, located in the engine compartment, has also been nickel plated. The fuel delivery rail has been plated with nickel-phosphorus.

Catalytic converter (stock)

1-liter volume, Pt:Rh loaded, close coupled to the exhaust manifold.

CPSIA information can be obtained at www.ICGtesting.com
Printed in the USA
BVOW04s0009220715

409716BV00014B/206/P